Wealth 101 for teenagers

Natalie Grignon, CDFA®

Dedication

To my children; being a mother made me want to be a good person for myself, for you and for my community.

To all of you whom I have met,

Whether you are currently part of my life or have been in the past; You helped shaped my life.

I am blessed & grateful.

ISBN: 978-1-9994684-0-8

© 2018 Natalie Grignon

Although the author has made every effort to ensure that the information in this book was correct at press time, the author does not assume and hereby disclaim any liability to any party for any loss, damage, or disruption caused by errors or omissions, whether such errors or omissions result from negligence, accident, or any other cause. The information in this book is meant to supplement, not replace, the advice given by your advisor.

Book design by: BDT Covers
Author Photograph by : Eva Ricci Studios

Contents

This book is separated into 4 parts : Budgeting, Inflation, Interest and Investments

Introduction

Budgeting :
    Chapter 1: Budget basics for the teenager with pocket money.
    Chapter 2 : For the teenager with a part-time job.
    Chapter 3: Creating a budget before living on your own
    Chapter 4 : My story

Inflation
    Chapter 5 : What is inflation
    Chapter 6 : Why it matters to teenagers
    Chapter 7 :To keep in mind for the future

Interest
    Chapter 8 : My story
    Chapter 9 : Interest and credit cards
    Chapter 10: Mortgages
    Chapter 11: The magic of compounding interest

Investments

    Chapter 12 : Why invest your money ?
    Chapter 13 : My story
    Chapter 14 : What are my investment choices ?
    Chapter 15 : What is a GIC
    Chapter 16: What is a mutual Fund ?
    Chapter 17: What is a stock ?
    Chapter 18 : What are the other choices ?. (ETF's , seg funds)

Chapter 19 : What is a RSP and TFSA ?
Chapter 20 : How to make sense of it all

Introduction

I was interested in writing this book because I meet many individuals who do not have the minimum knowledge of finance to achieve long-term financial success or to pass the knowledge off to the future generations.

All parents want their children to be happy and successful. Success is relative and goals are different, but for many, financial success simply means not having debt and living below their means. The Bank of Canada recently published that the average household debt in Canada is at 170% of disposable income. (source : https://www.bankofcanada.ca/2018/05/canada-economy-household-debt-how-big-the-problem/)

Too many young adults finish University with credit card debts and living above their means. The Instagram & YouTube generation is about showing on social media what a great life they lead. Trips, cars, mansions. My son knows details about cars like an accountant knows the tax laws, and he is only 15. The names he mentions are not his friends', but YouTube kids who put up memes and videos.

(or it might be Instagram memes and YouTube videos, hard to keep up) .

At 15 , he is already talking about buying his first car, moving into his own apartment, 'living the life', freedom & Starbucks. At this point, I try to give him a little reality check. I mentioned to him the other day that he needs consistent revenues, thus a steady job that he can count on. The price of an apartment, hydro, internet, cable, groceries, cellular phone, etc is at least $2000 per month.

If you are a teenager who is anxious to move out of your parent's place and be on your own, this is a book for you. This is the basic financial information you need to start your journey as a young adult, and to guide you make informed decisions onward.

Chapter 1

Budget basics for the teenager with pocket money.

What we call 'pocket money' is the small amount of money that you earn doing small jobs, like babysitting, or your weekly allowance.

Developing a good spending/saving habit now is crucial. Habits are formed from when we are younger, and they are harder to change.

Most advise to save 10% , without thinking, automatically, before spending on anything. This 10% saving habit is good. You could even try to raise it to 15% or 20%. Most importantly is to develop this habit. Where to put this money? Every major bank has a savings account for children. Most of the time there is no monthly fee, with a maximum of allowed transactions.

If you are saving for an Xbox or a new phone, your budget could look like this :

Monthly budget	amount	saving for Xbox	saving account	Tim Horton's	other
Allowance & babysitting	$ 60.00	$ 30.00	$ 6.00	$ 14.00	$ 10.00

The $6 savings might seem so little compared to the rest. If it does seem like a small amount to you, increase it to 15% or 20%.

Do not over-do it though, because the goal is to create a habit.

Having a saving habit that is realistic and painless will make you feel in control and you will be able to maintain it.

Here is an example of a busy month :

Month : December		saving for	saving		
Monthly budget	amount	Xbox	account	Tim Horton's	other
Allowance	$ 20.00	$ 6.00	$ 2.00	$ 10.00	$ 2.00
Babysitting	$ 30.00	$ 12.00	$ 3.00	$ 10.00	$ 5.00
Christmas gifts	$ 120.00	$ 48.00	$ 12.00	$ 50.00	$ 10.00
Birthday gift	$ 50.00	$ 15.00	$ 5.00	$ 20.00	$ 10.00
total for the month	$ 220.00	$ 81.00	$ 22.00	$ 90.00	$ 27.00

You could keep an excel sheet like this for future pocket change:

Month : January		saving for Xbox	saving account	Tim Horton's	other
Monthly budget	amount				
Allowance					
Babysitting					

'Developing a good spending/saving habit now is crucial'

Chapter 2   for the teenager with a part-time job.

There is one thing that you must do to take control of your finances.

A budget.

A realistic one.

Why ? because it is the basis of taking control of your finances. You must know your numbers.

Also, you cannot create a financial plan, thus plan where you want to go, without knowing where you are. It is the same principle as a GPS, it needs to know where you are going and where you are…….

Why are we talking about a Financial Plan while you are just a teenager? You might think Financial Plans are for people in their 40's, but you will understand later in the chapter about interest.

When creating a budget, keep in mind the following :

- If you have been in denial about your spending, this exercise might make you upset. It is ok, since we are not concentrating on the past. Create the budget and be ok with the outcome. Knowing the truth now is bringing you closer to your financial goals

- It will constantly be changing. You might have forgotten a few things, and you will eventually change numbers and add things. The trick is to keep in an Excel Sheet.

- There are some items that you are leaving out : like Christmas & birthday gifts, etc. Calculate those on a monthly basis. Example, if you spend $1500 on Christmas and birthday gifts, you should enter it as $125 per month.

- And be truthful about the rest. Those days that you were in a rush, and you stopped by Tim Horton's for breakfast. That water-bottle that you bought from your friend who is a Tupperware rep…..

- Things add up. If you go through your week without knowing how much pocket-money you have to spend, you will overspend. All week, all month, and all year.

'……..it is the basis of taking control of your finances. You must know your numbers.'

Chapter 3

Creating a budget before living on your own

You cannot wait to move out of your parents' place and be on your own ? As mentioned in Chapter 2, making a budget & knowing your numbers is crucial for having financial success, or at least not getting into financial troubles.

Take a look at the budget template on the next few pages, and here are the steps to creating a budget.

First : enter your biggest expenses. For most, there are 3 big ones;

Housing, transportation and groceries.

If , once you calculate these 3, you have reached most of your monthly income, you are in trouble. Why ? Because living expenses are much more than these 3.

Second: enter the fixed expenses that you cannot eliminate. Like hydro and car insurance. You can try to reduce these expenses, but you cannot eliminate fully.

Third : enter your expenses that you could eliminate,

but shouldn't , like life insurance.

Fourth : be realistic, these are your Starbucks coffees, restaurant and movie expenses, etc.

Here is an example of a budget.

(If you'd prefer to receive an Excel sheet by email

The Excel sheet has a more thorough budget)

	monthly amount
Biggest Expenses	
Housing (rent or mortgage) $750 total	
Transportation (car payment or other like bus pass)	
Groceries	
total	0

Cannot cancel	
Hydro	
Car insurance	
city, water, municipal taxes	
car license	
total	0

Could cancel, but necessary	
Life insurance	
Home insurance	
Gas	
Car repairs & maintenance	
Clothing	
total	0

Could cancel, but almost necessary	
phone & cell	
internet and cable	
total	0.00

Extras	
Restaurant (Mcdo or pizza)	
Gym membership	
Coffees (2,81$, every week day) not calculating tip	
accountant or professional fees	
hair & nails	
other, beer & parties (every weekend)	
total	0.00
Grand total	0

You will notice that I did not put credit card/ loan payments, nor daycare expenses. These are definitely part of the biggest expenses for some. Feel free to add, change or remove some things.

Case Study

> **Patrick**
>
> 19 yrs old
>
> $1100 net monthly income
>
> $1270 total monthly expenses

Here is an example. This was given to me by a 19 year old, let's call him Patrick. He says he is struggling financially, and accumulating debt, and wants some tips.

His revenue, working part-time (20 hours per week), is $1100 net per month. His parents still pay for his schooling,

and he does not qualify for student loans.

He decided to get an apartment with his friend. He thought it would be fun, living on his own. Leaving his parent's house was a choice, not a necessity (like moving closer to a college) .They share all the costs 50%, except their individual cell phones and bus passes.

Patrick's part of the costs — monthly amount

Biggest Expenses

Housing (rent or mortgage) $750 total	375
Transportation (car payment or other like bus pass)	120
Groceries	200
total	695

Cannot cancel

Hydro	75
Car insurance	
city, water, municipal taxes	
car license	
total	75

Could cancel, but necessary

Life insurance	
Home insurance	22
Gas	
Car repairs & maintenance	
Clothing	50
total	50

Could cancel, but almost necessary

phone & cell	90
internet and cable	110
total	200

Extras

Restaurant (Mcdo or pizza)	75
Gym membership	15
Coffees (2,81$, every week day) not calculating tip	60
accountant or professional fees	
hair & nails	
other, beer & parties (every weekend)	100
total	250
Grand total	1270

From first glance, you can tell that he is spending more than his $1100 revenue.

Patrick's housing cost of $750 per month is the average cost of a 2-bedroom apartment in some areas of Montreal, he wants to live in Lachine.

(source : https://montrealgazette.com/news/local-news/renters-rule-in-montreal-spending-an-average-835-monthly-on-housing)

> Tips for parent :
>
> Children follow
>
> in our footsteps…..
>
> Your budget should
>
> also be up to date

Possible recommendations:

stop spending on restaurants & coffee

stop the parties

But that is the whole reason to move out, right ?

Freedom, fun, and no one telling you what to do.

Other things to discuss :

- There is no life Insurance
- There is no savings

> **Possible solution #1 :**
>
> Get another roommate, thus sharing the costs with another person.

Patrick's part of the costs — monthly amount

Biggest Expenses

Housing (rent or mortgage) $750 total	
Transportation (car payment or other like bus pass)	120
Groceries	
total	120

Cannot cancel

Hydro	
Car insurance	
city, water, municipal taxes	
car license	
total	0

Could cancel, but necessary

Life insurance	
Home insurance	
Gas	
Car repairs & maintenance	
Clothing	50
total	50

Could cancel, but almost necessary

phone & cell	90
internet and cable	
total	90,00

Extras

Restaurant (Mcdo or pizza)	100
Gym membership	15
Coffees (2,81$, every week day) not calculating tip	60
accountant or professional fees	
hair & nails	
other, beer & parties (every weekend)	200,00
total	375,00
Grand total	635

Tips for parents :

Teenagers dream about the day they can move out.

Do not wait until they are 18 to start discussions on the cost of renting an apartment in your area.

Find out, by looking at KIJIJI, the cost of a one-bedroom or a two-bedroom.

Do not forget there is a difference in price with the following conditions :

-furnished, or not
-heated or not
-laundry room: in common area
(or inside the apartment)

The main take-away is the following: if you have a part-time job and are enjoying your Starbucks, movies, pizza and McDonald's, think really hard before adding the financial responsibilities of being on your own.

I had asked Patrick to review his options by thinking about the Pros and Cons. These are the lists he came up with:

Having 1 roommate

Pros:	Freedom from parents

Cons	Financial responsibility
	I have to pay full rent if roommate does not pay his part
	Credit score will go lower if roommate puts those payments on me
	Already getting myself into debt
	Roommate invites people I do not like
	Roommate has gotten into trouble with the law, in the past, afraid it will happen again

Getting a second roommate

Pros	Freedom from parents
	Second roommate helps pay for the costs

Cons	Financial responsibility
	If they both do not pay, I will have to pay it all
	Credit score risk still there
	Debt risk still there, if they both do not pay
	Second roommate is friend of first roommate (we could not agree on anyone else)
	They will both invite people I do not like
	Roommate #2, sketchy past
	He says he will never help clean bathroom

Going back to parents' house

Pros	Financial freedom
	Can start saving
	Can buy life insurance
	Will have money to go out
	Keeping a good credit score
	Accountable for my actions only
	Might be able to buy a car
	Will be able to travel
	Not afraid to be robbed in my own house by others
	Keeping up with the chores, I won't be alone doing them
	I can invite people I like

Cons	Not as much freedom

How did this story end? Patrick moved back home. It was not his idea to start with. His roommate did not want to follow his parent's rules and had begged Patrick to move in with him. Patrick realised he was too young to commit to those financial responsibilities.

Patrick was able to move back home. Not everybody is that lucky. If you are going to have a roommate or 2, keep in mind that you are sharing financial responsibilities with this person, and think of the possible scenarios :

-What if they decide to leave one morning ? (your answer will be: I will get another roommate. If this takes 1-2 months, can you pay everything yourself ?)

-What if they lose their jobs, can you pay everything ?

-What if one of you starts a serious committed-relationship and the significant other wants to move in?

-Do you have the same ethics, and share the same vision of this arrangement?
(example, quiet time during the week to be able to study, and 1 party on Friday nights)

-Who does what? Cooking, cleaning, grocery shopping, taking out the garbage, shoveling the entryway , etc.

-pets, or no pets?

-What if you get into a huge argument, one of you has to leave. Who will it be?

> Tips for parents:
>
> Do not convert his/her room into a gym just yet……
>
> Most children, who are still studying, come back home to live with their parents.
>
> Statistics Canada : Between 2001 and 2016, the share of young adults aged 20 to 34 who were living with at least one parent increased with each census.

'if you are enjoying your Starbucks, movies, pizza and McDonald's, think really hard before adding the financial responsibilities of being on your own'

Chapter 4: my story

My first job was a regular babysitting job for a couple with 2 children. It was a regular schedule, so I could count on the money coming in every week. This started the summer before my last year of high school, so I had planned to save up as much as possible for my grad. I had created a list of everything that I needed for my graduation, and I was dedicated to pay everything myself. From that point on, I never asked my mom for any money.

Here is the list of things that I wanted for my grad, and my total budget. (keep in mind that this was in the early 90's, and finding a dress below $200 was very doable).

Dress	200.00 $
Jewelry and purse	40.00 $
Shoes	30.00 $
Makeup	20.00 $
Grad ceremoney/diner ticket	100.00 $
Taxi , 2 way	30.00 $
total	420.00 $

I stuck to this list. When I saw that I was close to the amount that I needed, I allowed myself some expenses, like clothing.

This experience allowed me to set a long-term goal (1 year of saving is long for a teenager) , and I was proud on my graduation day that I had paid everything myself.

Summary :

If you are a teenager with pocket money, learn now the valuable lesson of creating & sticking to a budget. Saving 10% as a habit now will give you a good base for when you are working.

If you are a teenager looking forward to living on your own, make sure you know the real cost of living. Be realistic and consider the following:

- Create a budget, enter the cost of what you think living on your own will be . Creating a budget and knowing your numbers is the first step to showing your parents that you have thought it through.
- How much money you will need to make the initial move ? The first time you move out of your parent's house will be costly. Furniture, like a couch, kitchen table, appliances, etc, to the smallest things like utensils. Make a list, make sure you have enough saved up to make the initial purchases.
- Do not forget, depending on where you live, tenants are sometimes obligated to give 2-months' rent in advance.

- If you have no credit, or bad credit, you might need someone to co-sign for you. The person who co-signs has the responsibility to pay if you do not. Do not assume your parents or another loved-one will co-sign anything for you.

Inflation

Chapter 5 : What is inflation

Chapter 6 : why it matters to teenagers

Chapter 7 :to keep in mind for the future

Chapter 5, what is inflation ?

This is the simplest explanation of inflation :

	June 2017	June 2018
Cost of groceries	$ 100	$ 102.22

In June 2018, your groceries cost you 2.22% more than in 2017.

Here are the inflation rates of the past years :

As shown on the Bank of Canada website, the inflation is calculated from September of one year to September of the next year.

Year	Inflation
2016	1.55
2015	1.34
2014	1.03
2013	2.03
2012	1.07
2011	1.16
2010	3.17

Ref : https://www.bankofcanada.ca/rates/related/inflation-calculator/

The Bank of Canada aims to keep inflation at the 2 % midpoint of an 'Inflation-control target' range of 1 to 3 %.

The **Bank of Canada** is Canada's central bank.

Its mandate is to promote the economic and financial welfare of Canadians.

It has 4 core functions:

- Monetary Policy
- Financial System
- Currency
- Funds management

The inflation is controlled under the Monetary Policy.

> Myth :
>
> Some people think that the 'cost of living' is the same as inflation. They are closely related, but not the same.

Inflation is a bigger picture, and measured by the Consumer Price Index (CPI). The CPI averages the cost of goods and services that Canadians buy, such as food, housing, transportation, and other items. The inflation rate quoted in Montreal is the same quoted in Toronto.

The **Cost of Living** is more focused. It is used to compare life in different locations. For example you will hear that the cost of living in Toronto is more expensive than in Montreal.

For example, a one-bedroom apartment in Toronto is $1400 compared to $900 in Montreal. That is 55% more. *

An average detached home in Toronto is $1.2 million, compared to $325,000 in Montreal.*

(* from Workopolis website October 2016)

More information on inflation :

https://www.bankofcanada.ca/core-functions/monetary-policy/inflation/

Chapter 6 : why it matters to teenagers?

It matters, a lot, to some teenagers. Did it ever happen to you, to have the exact change to buy an Ice Cap from Tim Horton's , to find out that they raised the price ? That is inflation.

The price of goods go up, or the quantity goes down. Did you ever notice your favorite brand of peanut butter went from 1Kg to 920g ? The price did not go up, but they did reduce the size of the jar. That is inflation.

Are you saving up for many years for a scooter ? Since you were 13 and looking at scooter prices, the price went up. A $2000 scooter 3 years ago is probably around $2120 today. Not a big deal ? Think about it, everything that you are buying today, from movie tickets, to coffee and clothing, everything will be more expensive next year. (and the years after that)

And what about a car? You cannot wait to buy your own car , but did you notice that the price quoted on your favorite car is a tad higher today ?

Chapter 7 : keep in mind for the future….

      i)   For jobs
      ii)   Savings

    i)   Why inflation is something to think about when you are job-hunting………

Some of the people I have met told me that they did not get a raise in the past 5 or more years. If you really think about it, inflation goes up about 2% per year. This means that your purchasing power is lower every year that your salary stays the same.

They also told me that they feel poorer today than a few years ago, they have more debt and cannot seem to get a handle of their finances.

Keep this in mind for when you are looking for your dream job and have a couple of offers. You might want to choose the job that offers bonuses and yearly raises.

ii) Why is inflation important to consider when you start saving ?

We mentioned that the inflation stays between 1 and 3 % , and the Bank of Canada tries to keep it around 2%.

If you save $100, and leave it in a savings account for a few years making less than 1% interest, your $100 will be worth less today than a few years ago.

Instead of just leaving money in a savings account, start investing. In the next chapter, you will understand the magic of compound interest.

Summary:

Inflation is an element we take into consideration when creating a financial plan for a client.

Do not forget that a stagnant salary or bank account will make you poorer in the long-run

Interest

Chapter 8 : my story

Chapter 9 : interest and credit cards

Chapter 10: mortgages

Chapter 11: the magic of compounding interest

Chapter 8 : My Story

When I was in elementary school, about 8 or 9 years old, I was confused about the word interest, especially people's reaction and feelings when they would talk about it. Let me explain. Most of the time, I would hear comments like:

' I am paying so much interest'

Or

'I hate that my interest rate is so high'

I understood that. We pay interest on money we borrow. Like credit cards or loans.

The following comment left me confused:

' yay, I received my interest today' .

So , for a little while, I was confused about interest. I was questioning is it good or bad ?

Then I learned about investments. How your money saved in an account can grow , with interest or dividends. Finally I understood, you **pay** interest when you borrow money, like when you use a credit card to buy something. You **receive** interest when the bank 'borrows' your money. Well, the bank or another borrower, like an investment. (Investments discussed in the next chapters.)

Chapter 9 : interest and credit cards

Credit cards can be useful to buy something online or to book trips. Here are the questions I receive the most from teenagers:

1) What is exactly is a credit card ?
2) How do I get a credit card?
3) Why do we keep hearing about credit score or having no credit ? What exactly is that ?
4) Why do people get into trouble with credit cards ?
5) What is the limit to how much I can spend ? Is it limitless ?
6) Why do some people have so many cards ?

What is exactly a credit card ?

Most teenagers have used a debit card in the past, but are not sure about the difference about a debit card or credit card.

A debit card: when you open up a bank account, you receive a debit card. When you make a transaction, like to buy a coffee, the amount is debited from your bank account (deducted) . You have to know exactly how much money you have left in your bank account before you make a purchase.

A credit card uses a limit. Let's say your limit is $500.

You can make purchases up to $500.

The amount is not deducted from your bank account, but you will owe the credit card company.

At the end of the month, you will receive a credit card statement showing your transactions and amount that you owe.

You do not have to pay the total amount that you owe right away.

The credit card company will ask you for a minimum payment. You have to pay at least the minimum.

The amount, either partial or full, must be paid within a specified delay.

Interest is then added on to any unpaid balance. The interest rate can be as high as 21%.

How do I get a credit card?

You have to apply to get a credit card. You might get a 'pre-approved' letter in the mail, or even by email from your bank.

Most people apply for credit cards online.

The application approval will depend on your current job status, your salary and your credit score.

Why do we keep hearing about credit score or having no credit ? What exactly is that ?

You credit score is a number ranging from 300 to 900.

The lower the number, the worst your score is.

Having no credit is not as bad as having bad credit, but it might keep you from being able to apply for credit.

Credit scores and reports are based on your personal information and this information is kept by companies called Credit Bureaus. Credit Bureaus are companies that collect information on people and their credit ratings. They only share this information to credit card companies, financial institutions and other companies when you apply for a loan or credit.

It is important to contact the Credit Bureaus if you think there is wrong information in your file, and even identity theft.

You can contact these companies to get your credit score and your report. Some banks give you your credit score for free.

You keep your score high :

- by always paying your bills, on time
- have low debt compared to your income

It is important to keep a good credit score. Purchases like a car and a home will be harder with bad scores.

Even your dream job application might be denied because of a bad credit history.

Keep in mind that when you apply for things like a car loan or your dream apartment, they might check other things besides the credit score, like criminal history or rental board.

Why do people get into trouble with credit cards ?

The reason why people get into trouble with credit cards is that they spend more than what they can really afford. In the example above, the credit limit is only $500. What if your credit card limit is $2000 and you have reached it.

Can you pay back $2000 quickly to avoid interest charges ?

If you cannot, you will end up only paying a portion of the total, and then interest will start adding on.

Also, most people have more than 1 credit card. You end up only paying the minimum payments, or borrowing from your Visa to pay the minimum of your MasterCard.

Example :

- Credit card debt of $500
- Interest rate : 18.9 %
- Minimum payment of $20
- Will take 11 years to pay it off (if you only pay the minimum monthly amount)

What is the limit to how much I can spend ? Is it limitless ?

We have all heard of limitless, exclusive credit cards.
Yes, they do exist, but for only the elite few.
For most of us, we have a limit.

Most college students tell me that their first credit card had a limit of $500. And this limit was reached fast, with restaurants, clothing and outings to the movie theatre.

The trick is to use the credit card during the month, and then pay back at the end of the month when you receive your paycheck.

Why do some people have so many cards ?

As long as your credit score is good, your credit card applications might all be approved.

Then, you end up with multiple cards.

After, there is always an emergency:

- I need clothing for my aunt's wedding.
- I need to buy a lunch between my 2 classes because I forgot my lunch at home.
- It is my friend's birthday and I need to buy something nice.
- Everyone is going on vacation, so I want to go as well.

People apply for credit cards when they feel they are running out of money, or their other cards are full. They then start a vicious cycle.

Chapter 10: mortgages

What is my favorite question to ask teenagers? How much do houses cost? Some know exactly how much they are because they had a conversation with their parents, or were curious enough and looked it up themselves.

Some have answered me $5,000 or $50,000. When I say a regular-family bungalow in my area is around $400,000, some of them have a huge reaction. Why the huge reaction? They think you have to pay cash.

No need to pay cash, we have access to mortgages.

What are mortgages?

- A mortgage is a loan, mostly from banks.
- It is calculated on a 25-year payment plan. (you can chose less years)
- We do not set a fixed interest rate for those 25 years.
- Most use 5-year periods. (you can use smaller periods)
- You can have a **fixed** rate of return for those 5 years. (fixed: means it does not change for the 5 years)
- Or a **variable** rate of return.
- Variable means that it goes up or down depending on the actual rate.
- Most people chose fixed when they think the rates will go up, and soon.

- Most people who chose variable is because they think they have time before the rates will go up, or the rates are going lower.
- To get a mortgage, the banks will look at your credit score, your salary, etc.
- You need to have a cash-down to be eligible for a mortgage. This means that you have money to deposit into the purchase of the home. The home cannot be 100% financed through the mortgage.
- Most people have a cash-down of 5-10%

For example, a $400,000 house needs a cash-down of $20,000.

But when buying a house, there are fees, like the notary fees and the 'welcome tax ' (the city where you are buying the house will welcome you into the neighborhood with a tax, called the 'welcome tax') no kidding…..

When buying your first home, the bank might ask you if you have someone who can co-sign. A co-signer is someone responsible to make your payments if you do not.

In Canada, we have a program that helps you buy a home. It is called Home Buyer's Plan. This plan allows you to withdraw up to a certain amount from your RSP account to buy or build a home. In 2018, this amount is $25,000.

Check with your advisor if there is a similar program in your country.

If your goal is to buy a home in the next few years, discuss and plan with your advisor as soon as you can.

Chapter 11 : the magic of compounding interest

The simplest way to explain the magic of compound interest was given by the Stanton University back in the 1960's, and the study has been known as the 'Marshmallow Test'. [1. (https://jamesclear.com/delayed-gratification)]

Preschool children were given 2 choices :

You can have ONE marshmallow right now

OR

Wait 20 minutes and you will have 2

What happened to those children?

Did they understand the principal of delayed gratification?

Standford's study shows that years later; the children who waited for the second Marshmallow did better in life.

Makes sense. Why ? Because if you are a person who needs instant gratification, you will buy that purse or game on credit, instead of saving up for it. We live in a society that uses credit not for emergencies, but for the 'I want in now '.

If you are thinking that 2 marshmallows instead of 1 is not a big deal, remember that the children had to wait only 20 minutes.

If you want to grow your money to eventually buy a house, your dream car or to fund your retirement, compound interest will be what you'll count on.

Another simple way to explain the magic of compound interest :

(not considering fees nor inflation)

Step 1:

You have $100

With interest rate of 2%

You will have $102 by the end of the first year.

Step 2:

Then, the next year, you have $102

And the interest will be calculated on $102, not $100

And so forth.

Still not a big deal ? I used simple numbers, $100 and 2%. But what if the amount is bigger, and the interest rate is more important ?

Consider the Rule of 72 [2]

This quick calculation allows you to know how many years it will take to double your money.

72 ÷ compound annual interest rate = the number of years it will take to double your money.

And this is what it looks like when the interest rate is higher

Years	1.5%	3%	6%	12%
0	$10,000	$10,000	$10,000	$10,000
6				$20,000
12			$20,000	$40,000
18				$80,000
24		$20,000	$40,000	$160,000
30				$320,000
36			$80,000	$640,000
42				$1,280,000
48	$20,000	$40,000	$160,000	$2,560,000

[2] Albert Einstein discovered this rule of 72. He thought compounding interest was even more important to understand than his formula $E=MC^2$

So, Would you rather have $20,000 or $2,560,000 ?

No one is guaranteeing a 12 % return, unless it is a guaranteed investment, to be discussed in the next chapters.

Keep those numbers in mind, because it is as true with interest on investments or on credit.

Summary :

If you want to have financial success in life, make sure that interest is working for you, not against you.

Investments

Chapter 12 : Why invest your money ?

So if you remember a few pages back, (the rule of 72) the numbers are enormously different. Ask anyone if they would rather have $20,000 or $2,560,000;

the answer will always be $2,560,000.

However, what do you feel when I tell you that the $2,560,000 is not a guarantee and not without risk.

This risk is why not everyone is invested in the Stock Market.
(Stock Market described in Chapter 17)

The fear of losing the original $10,000 keeps people in that first column .

The next few chapters give you the basic information on investments.

Chapter 13

My story : my first thoughts about investments

When people ask me about my story, (because people are always curious about why/how people decided to pursue this career) , I often tell them this funny story :

When I was 12, someone mentioned the story of how someone became rich with their Pepsi shares, that they had purchased Pepsi for pennies, and now worth millions.

I was 12 and thought I knew a lot about the world already , but it was the first time I had heard about 'shares', or 'stocks' or 'equity'. My first questions were :

1) How come I do not know anyone who owns 'shares' of anything ?
2) At what age can I buy ?
3) How come not everyone is buying and becoming rich ?

First of all, I come from a very poor family. My mom has 10 siblings, and they did not see toothpaste until their late teens, much less know anything about shares of a public company.

Second, you have to be 18 to have your own investment account and be able to buy shares.

And lastly, not everyone becomes rich from buying stocks. I have met a lot of people who have invested a fortune in the Stock market and lost. Then, it follows to ask : why would I then invest in the Stock Market ?

Have you heard the expression 'do not put all your eggs in the same basket'? This applies to investing. If you have $20,000 saved and want to invest, would you want to risk it all with the hope of making a big return? Or would you rather invest in something with less risk with a smaller return?

Most people are in between. They want their money to grow, in the long-run, but understand the risk short-term. And what does that mean exactly?

Let's say you are 18 and you know that you want to save to buy a house in 5-8 years, and you also want to start saving for retirement. You already know that at retirement, you will want to travel the world, so you'll need a lot of money.

Buying a house is a shorter-term goal. You will want your savings to grow, but cannot afford to get hit by a bad drop.

Retirement is many years away; you will want your money to grow. Even if it drops, because of declining markets, you will have enough years to catch it up.

Chapter 14

What are my investment choices?

There are 3 main investment choices:

- GIC's   (guaranteed investment certificates)

- mutual funds

- stocks

However, what you can buy in your investment account depends on where your investment account is, (which institution/ firm).

I will give you 2 examples :

At the bank :

The bank can only offer you mutual funds and GIC's.

At a securities firm:

GIC's, mutual funds, stocks, ETF'x, Options, etc can be purchased through a securities firm.

Why then bother with opening an account with a bank when a securities firm can offer more options ? Here are the 2 main reasons :

-Most securities firms have a minimum investment for their accounts, of $100,000 or more.

-There are fees with their accounts, either a flat fee, like $50 -$125, per account, or a fixed 2% management fee.

Therefore, some might decide to keep their money at the bank until it has reached a sizeable amount, then move on to a securities firm.

Chapter 15 : What is a GIC

- A GIC is one the simplest things to invest in.
- They are Guaranteed Investment Certificates.
- The money you invest (called your capital) is guaranteed.
- A traditional GIC has a fixed interest rate that you will receive on top of your capital.
- There is always a maturity date
- It might be cashable or not before maturity

So for example,

- 1 yr GIC with 5% rate
- purchased on Oct 31 2017
- with $1000.

On Oct 31 2018, this is the maturity date.
You will receive $1050

Besides the traditional GIC, you can purchase some variations, here are 2 examples :

<u>Market-Linked</u> :   - your principal is still guaranteed
                             -rate of return is linked to the performance of the Stock market

<u>Variable rate</u> :   - your principal is still guaranteed
                             - rate of return is linked to a benchmark, for example the bank's prime rate

When I explain what a GIC is to a teenager, I get the following question : If a GIC is guaranteed , it means that there is no risk, should I invest all of my money in that ?

If this was 1981, many people would say yes. London Life[3] has published a chart with the following numbers :

Year	5-year GIC
1980	12.3 %
1981	15.4%
2008	3.0%
2009	1.9%

So , as you can see, the GIC rates have gone down.

When this happens, people invest their money in other products like Mutual Funds or Stocks.

[3] https://www.ratehub.ca/blog/the-history-of-gic-rates/)

Chapter 16: what is a mutual Fund ?

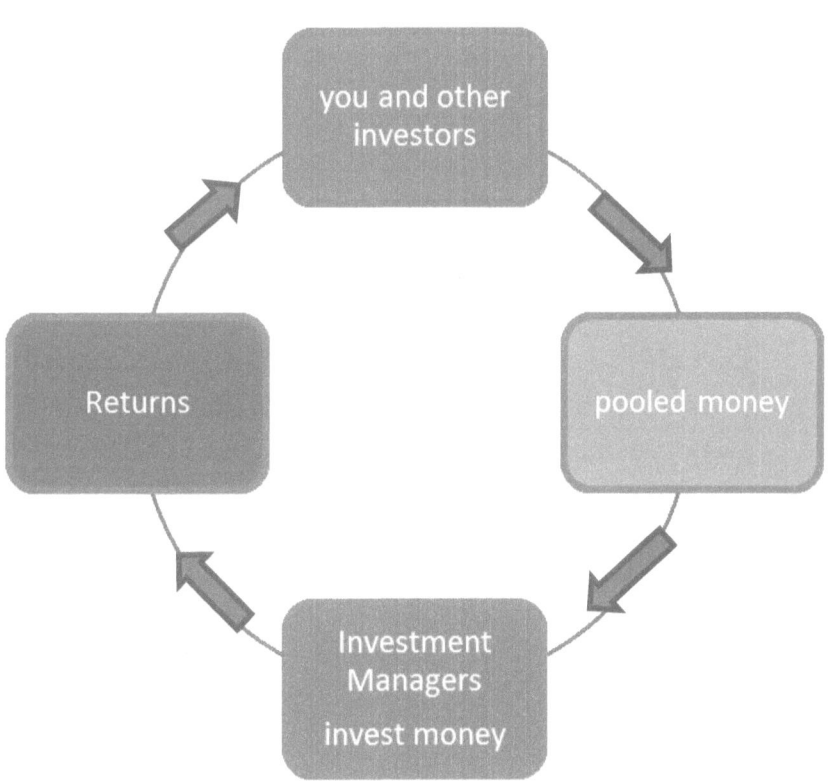

-Your money is pooled with other people's money.

-The Investment Manager of that pool purchases securities

-You do not own the individual securities, you own units of the mutual fund.

-There are many mutual funds to choose from

-The name of the fund gives a clue as how the mutual fund is invested in.

Example : Canadian Dividend Growth Fund: the fund will invest in Canadian Companies , and only companies which give out a dividend.

How do I know which mutual fund to buy ?

The good news is: even though there are so many funds to choose from, your advisor is there to help you.

Advisors have the obligation to ask you questions to see your tolerance to risk. When he/she will recommend a mutual fund, or another investment, it will be based on a few factors including the risk tolerance.

If you do not know much about the market or the investments, I do not recommend that you make your own investment choices.

Can I really start investing with only $25 per month ?

Yes, with mutual funds, you can start with as little as $25 per month. You can have a portion of a unit.

For example:

you are buying into a Canadian Growth Fund

the fund is currently at $9.50 per unit

You invest $25

You own : 2.632 units

Chapter 17: What is a stock ?

A stock, or share, is ownership of a public company.

Did you know that you could own shares of Starbucks, Apple, or Facebook? They are all Public Companies.

A 'public company' : the public can buy shares in an open market, like the Toronto Stock Exchange (TSX).

A 'private company' : the public cannot buy shares on an open market. An example of a private company is your corner mom-and-pop- store, which is owned by husband and wife.

How can I start buying stocks ?

- You need to be 18 to purchase investments in an account in your name.
- To have an account with an Investment Advisor in a securities firm, you must qualify to open the account. (because most Securities Firms have minimum investment minimums)
- You can purchase stocks from a self-directed investing app. Most of the time these apps charge a $10 fee per transaction. You have to make your own investing decisions. You are completely on your own with these apps, no one will advise you to buy, sell or hold.

Making money from Stocks is a sure thing ?

No, it is not a 'sure-thing', but here are things to know :

- Your money invested in stocks is not guaranteed
- In the long-run, the Stock Market has offered the most growth compared to the other investments
- There are 2 ways to make money from stocks : trading and investing . (trading is watching the market , and knowing what and when to buy/sell. Investing is buying stocks of companies that you think will grow in the long run. Thus buying and holding.)
- One way to lose money is to react like the people around you. Most people sell in a panic and buy when there is hype. You should do the opposite.

- Another way to lose money is to buy a 'Penny-Stock'. Most people think that Penny Stocks are trading below $1 , but it is all stocks trading below $5 with a very low volume. You will often hear 'buy this penny stock for 20 cents, for sure it will go up'. Nothing is for sure. A penny stock is always a speculation.
- Stay away from an Investment Advisor who is pushing a Penny Stock. The 'Pump and Dump' is sometimes used by Investment Advisors who are sleazy. Even though there are very strict rules and regulations, it could happen.
- A 'pump and dump' is an illegal strategy to make money from penny stocks :
    1. The advisor buys a penny stock for his own personal accounts
    2. Buys in his clients' accounts to make the price go higher.
    3. Then sells his shares

- Work with an Investment Advisor who you are comfortable with. He/she will explain the investment strategy that is used.

Chapter 18 : What are the other investment choices ?

You want to start investing, but you want to know what else is there besides GIC's, mutual funds and stocks?

There are a few other investment products you can invest in : like Segregated funds, ETF's and Options.

Segregated funds :

- Similar to mutual funds.
- Money is pooled with other investors.
- They are offered by insurance companies.
- Sometimes have guarantees at death and maturity.
- Could be a protection against creditors (a creditor is someone you owe money to)
- Investment is passed onto named beneficiaries at death
- The guarantees come at a price, money is locked-in and has higher MER fees (MER fees are the fees paid to the investment managers). There are also penalties for withdrawing before maturity date.
- You can often start with as little as $25 or $50 per month.

ETF's

- Exchange-traded funds
- Similar to mutual funds, but traded on the markets like a stock
- Have MER fees like a mutual fund, but are lower.
- When you trade an ETF, the price is known as soon as the transaction is done. A mutual fund, the price is calculated at the end of the day.
- Since it is traded like a stock, banks cannot offer.

Options

- A stock option is a contract between 2 parties
- Option buyer has the right (but not the obligation) to buy /sell 100 shares of a specific stock at a specific price within a fixed period of time.
- You do not hold the stock, you hold the 'option' to buy or sell.
- Option to buy the specific stock : a Call Option
- Option to sell the specific stock : a Put Option
- You are not paying the price of the stock, you are paying a premium

Example :

- You want to buy Royal Bank shares.
- You think the price of the Royal Bank shares will go up in the next few months, but do not feel confident enough to buy the shares now.
- You buy a Call option with maturity date of July 19 2019.
- With a strike price of $92.
- July 2019 is 7 months away
- and Royal Bank is trading right now at $91.
- You pay a premium , of $4.85, for this option.
- So the total cost right now is $485 for 1 contract.
- (1 contract is 100 shares, so the premium price of $4.85 x 100 shares)

So you purchased the option at $485 instead of paying $9100 for 100 shares of Royal Bank.

If the price drops instead of going up and you do not exercise your option, your loss is $485.

But what if the shares go up ?

In June 2019, you notice that the Royal Bank shares are trading at $120 per share.

You decide to exercise your Call Option (thus buying 100 shares at $92), and right away turning around to sell at the market price of $120 in the same day.

This is your profit :

December 2018	Price for the option	$485
June 2019	Exercise the option	$9,200
	Total cost of shares	$9,685
June 2019	Sell shares same day	$12,000
	Total profit :	$2,315

Summary

*There are plenty of investment options to choose from.
If you are inexperienced &
have little money to invest,
your first choice will probably
be mutual funds.*

*Starting to save & invest
is a step more important
than understanding the markets and
individual investments.*

Chapter 19 : What is a RSP and TFSA ?

So, you are ready to start saving, now what ?

You probably heard people talking about cash accounts, RSP and TFSA. What are they, how do I know where to start investing ?

Here is a brief description, with the pros and cons for each.

Before explaining each account, you have to understand the difference between a 'registered' and 'non-registered' account.

Registered Account :

- Regulated by the government
- Contributions & withdrawals are verified by the government, and there are limits to the amount you can contribute/withdraw
- There are penalties for not following the contribution rules.
- Money grows tax-free
- All income: interest & dividends are received tax-free

>Example, you deposit $1000.
>Your account grows to $1400
>The $400 is tax-free

Non-registered account:

- Also known as a cash account.
- You can withdraw & deposit as much as you want
- No maximum account size
- All gains & revenues in the account is taxable

If there are no restrictions in the cash account, why would anyone open any other types of accounts?

See next pages for pros and cons of each account.

RSP

- Registered Savings Plan
- In some firms, you must be 18 years old or older to open this account
- The contributions limit (the amount of money you can put in) is calculated in function of your earned income from the previous year.
- The calculation is 18% of last year's earned income
- The calculation also includes Pension Plan contributions and adjustments (but forget those numbers for now)
- There is an annual limit , for example, in 2019 it is $26,500
- You do not lose your contribution room.
  (thus the limit is important to watch out for if you maximise every year)
- Do not worry if you did not keep track, Canada Revenue Agency keeps track and you see those numbers in your online file.
- Designed primarily to save towards your retirement

- Since it is registered, it grows tax-free
- Contributions can greatly reduce your income taxes payable. (when you do your income taxes, the amounts contributed in your RSP is deductible)
- A portion can be used to buy your first home.
- A portion can also be used for Lifelong Learning
- The year that you turn 71, you have to decide what to do with your RSP :
    - Withdraw all of it (not the goal of most people because it is then fully taxable)
    - Convert it into an account which will give you a monthly payment (it is called a RRIF account – Registered Retirement Income Fund).
    - Buy an annuity. An annuity is an insurance product which gives you monthly payments. While interest rates are low, people tend to stay away from annuities.

Cons :

- There are fees and income taxes deducted if you withdraw while it is a RSP. (thus if you contribute to your RSP but use it as a cash account by withdrawing often, you will not see the advantages of a RSP) .
- If you make more than $150,000 per year, you will reach the maximum contribution allowed. ($150,000 * 18% is $27,000.)
- If you over-contribute there is a penalty (of 1% of the over-contribution per month.)
- Tax-free while you accumulate, but it will be taxable once you start withdrawing. If you convert it to a RIF at the age of 71 and take out only the minimum, the financial institution will not withdraw any taxes, but it will be included as income when you do your income tax return.

TFSA

- Tax Free Savings Account
- Registered, so it grows tax-free (any gain or revenue is not taxable. For example : you contribute $1000, the account grows to $2500. The $1500 growth is not taxable.)
- Can withdraw anytime
- Maximum contribution amount, the same for everyone. In 2019 it is $6000
- You must be 18
- The year you turn 18 you are allowed to contribute.
- The room is cumulative. For example: you turn 18 in 2018 , but do not have the $5500 (the maximum allowed in 2018) . In 2019 , you can contribute $11,500.
- Can open many TFSA's, but the maximum contribution has to be respected
- The amount that you withdraw this year can be re-contributed next year.

Cons :

- If you over-contribute , there is a penalty fee of 1% per month (on the over-contribution)
- If you withdraw this year, (and you had always maximised your account) , you have to be vigilant not to recontribute that amount this year. You have to wait until Jan 1st of the next year.
- Even though you can withdraw anytime, have the discussion with your advisor to see if your money will be invested in something that will incur fees at withdrawal.

Summary

You will often hear people complain about the taxes with RSP withdrawals.
Most of the time it is because they used their RSP account as a cash account.

To be successful with investing,
you have to <u>think of your RSP
as your retirement fund</u>
(not to be touched to buy a car
or plan a trip),

and your <u>TFSA as a 'what-if' account.</u>
- What if the roof needs to be redone?
- What if I get sick and do not have insurance?

You do not have to decide which account is better for you right now, or if you need both. Have the discussion with your advisor.

> *Tips for parents:*
>
> *Even if you had a bad experience with an investment, fees or penalties, have an open discussion with your teenager about his/her choices.*
>
> *Everyone's situation is different, so what was not recommended for you might be a good solution for his/her financial plan.*
>
> *The key is to know the pros and cons of each type of account or investment, and then making a calculated decision.*

Chapter 20 : how to make sense of it all

Before writing this chapter, I was thinking of my 15-year-old son. How will he grab all of this information and make sense of it all?

Will he use all of this info and have a financially successful life ?

I have two daughters as well, and I am not as concerned with them. Why ? Because my daughters have not been as obsessed with what they see on Instagram and Youtube. (well, if they are, they do not talk about it) They do not repeatedly talk about how they cannot wait to move out and be on their own. My son keeps thinking that with a part-time job and /or student loans , he will be able to live on his own. I do not get that. The cost of living is high.

He is good at math, but somehow does not seem to grasp how expensive it is to live on your own. If you spend more than you make, you will be in debt. Credit cards are not to be used to live a glamour life. This will get you in trouble.

Ok, so my son might be embarrassed by this if he reads this book. Sorry dude, you are just an example of all of the teenagers I come across who have a distorted view on how far a dollar can stretch.

What do you do with a teenager whose view of success is a 20 year-old-kid with a Lambo on Instagram ?

I have done workshops in the past with teenagers and their parents. In the workshop I discuss the same things as in this book. I absolutely love to do this. One of my goals this year is to have a frank discussion about Instagram and how real/unreal it seems to them. Lambos and mansions are not the norm for young adults, I hope they understand that much.

Rome was not built in a day- one of my favorite quotes.

Building wealth takes a long time.

Yes, you will hear stories of someone selling an App or a website for millions, it does happen, it is rare, but you will definitely hear that story.
You will also hear stories of a kid who made millions selling socks on Facebook, or someone making millions trading options.

But there are many other stories of how people went bankrupt, lost money in penny stocks, etc.

One thing I never did : compared myself to others. Don't try to imitate your friends or neighbors. If they bought a new car, good for them. Your friends all seem to be going on trips? Oh well, great. Do your own stuff.

Conclusion

By reading this book, I hope you have learned enough about budgeting, interest rates, inflation & investments to make informed decisions. As a teenager and young adult, the savings habit you create now will shape your future.

www.ingramcontent.com/pod-product-compliance
Lightning Source LLC
Chambersburg PA
CBHW030529080526
44586CB00011B/376